Thank you so m[uch] saying cheesing [you] as you [go] through ←

My Daily Clarity

90 Days to Connect.Create.Communicate.Celebrate

Nina Obier- BE the Leader of YOUR Life!

My Daily Clarity- 90 Days to Connect.Create.Communicate.Celebrate

Copyright © 2016 Nina Obier. All rights reserved.

Limits of Liability and Disclaimer of Warranty

The author and publisher shall not be liable for your misuse of this material. This book is strictly for informational and educational purposes.

Warning- Disclaimer
The purpose of this book is to educate and entertain. The author and publisher do not guarantee that anyone following these techniques, suggestions, tips, ideas, or strategies will become successful. The author and publisher shall have neither liability nor responsibility to anyone with respect to any loss or damage caused or alleged to be caused, directly or indirectly, by the information contained in this book.

WANT TO REPRINT A PORTION OF THIS BOOK ON YOUR BLOG, WEBSITE OR E-ZINE?

You're welcome to- just please include this complete blurb with it, thank you!

As a Thought Leader, Speaker and Coach in Human Communication Nina Obier specializes in teaching entrepreneurs to make more money more easily while enjoying the business and lifestyle that reflects their priorities. The time is now to Connect, Create, Communicate and Celebrate. Download Nina's "3 Simple Steps to Take Back YOUR Morning" now at www.NinaObier.com.

TITLE ID: 6738695
ISBN-13: 978-1540568847

ACKNOWLEDGMENTS

I am forever grateful to Dana Wilde of The Mind Aware for offering me the opportunity to be a part of her By Your Side program as an expert coach. The women who I have been blessed to meet have been such a gift to me both personally and professionally. Thank you so very much for reminding me everyday how much I love what I do!

My Daily Clarity- 90 Days to Connect.Create.Communicate.Celebrate

www.ninaobier.com

My Daily Clarity- 90 Days to Connect.Create.Communicate.Celebrate

Introduction

Here's everything you need to know about me, Nina Obier: I love ice cream, I'm a crazy fan of softball, I use the phrase "in my humble opinion" a lot, I'm passionate about personal development and I am known for having the wisdom of a 90 year old with the energy of a 9 year old. My personal mission is to be a role model and guide in #LeadingALifeOfHarmony.

What would having clarity mean to you? For me, it's everything. Do you ever have a foggy feeling? Or a feeling of overwhelm because you have too much going on in your head? Or too many things to do?

This simple yet powerful tool can be integrated into your life daily.

It encourages you to do some sort of braindump or journaling every day. From your findings you can then pick out the "big things" (like Steven Covey suggests in the 7 Habits of Highly Effective People- The Big Rocks)

You take your findings and focus on 4 areas every single day, Connect, Create, Communicate, Celebrate. These areas will mean something different for each of us.

I also include a tally that you mark to make sure you are staying hydrated. YES, hydration has been linked to clarity!

It's as simple as 1, 2, 3

1. Get the ideas out of your head.
2. Focus on 4 key areas: Connect, Create, Communicate, Celebrate
3. Stay hydrated and have the clarity YOU desire.

My Daily Clarity- 90 Days to Connect.Create.Communicate.Celebrate

But First, Let's Do a Braindump, Get it ALL out of Your Head
Date:_____(what's on your mind, what's on your calendar, what are your responsibilities, dreams, goals, vision, mission, let it all out)

_____
_____
_____
_____
_____
_____
_____
_____
_____
_____
_____
_____
_____
_____
_____
_____
_____
_____
_____
_____
_____
_____
_____
_____
_____
_____
_____
_____
_____
_____
_____
_____

My Daily Clarity- 90 Days to Connect.Create.Communicate.Celebrate

(Keep Going) Date: _____

My Daily Clarity- 90 Days to Connect.Create.Communicate.Celebrate

A Way of Life (braindump from 1-7-2016)

TAKE BACK YOUR LIFE!
Be Well Rounded
JOY in Everything!
Say NO, make room for YES!
Write Your Story
Connect with Yourself and Others
Create Moments- The Life You Love and The Change You Want to See
Communicate with Certainty, Clarity, and Compassion it Creates Partnerships
Simplify
Choose Grace
Pray
Make a Difference
Leave the World a Better Place
Smile
Listen.Learn.Love.Lead.Leave a Legacy…
Journal, Gratitude, Blessings
Be an Example
Powerful Force For Good in the World!

My Daily Clarity- 90 Days to Connect.Create.Communicate.Celebrate

Results From the Braindump:

My life is much more full now that there is less in it.

My Daily Clarity form was created, and now the book!

3 Simple Steps for your Morning Routine came to life. Which included a video series and these journal prompts: Today I AM. I Say YES to, I'm so Fired Up. I'm feeling so Cheerful & Blessed, I visualize Myself Being/Doing/Having, I'm Confident That, I'm Enthusiastic About & Devoted to Practicing

I collaborated on several projects over the year.

I met with my Power of 3 mastermind group every single month.

I traveled to as many college softball games as I could. Especially the one where my daughter's team became the conference champions.

I enjoyed going to concerts with my older daughter. Especially the one where she treated us to the VIP experience.

I consistently held my monthly Freedom Finders Connect Group where we continued to develop both personally and professionally.

I became a Partner for Pace, which supports the Pace Center for Girls in our county.

I joined the John Maxwell Group to become a certified speaker, trainer and coach.

I hosted two colleagues at my home for a retreat.

My Daily Clarity- 90 Days to Connect.Create.Communicate.Celebrate

Let's Get Technical

I get to thank google for offering these simple definitions and synonyms to bring the Four Areas of Daily Clarity to life.

Connect- to join (2 or more) together. To join with or become joined to something else. Synonyms- bridge, unite, plug into.

The connect step for me is all about mind, body, spirit. It is a time to listen, soul search and move. I do at least one of the following every single day: meditate, pray, read, devotional, journal, braindump, stretch, exercise, hydrate, vision, mission, purpose.

Create- bring something into existence. Cause (something) to happen as a result of one's actions. Synonyms- produce, generate, bring into being.

The create step for me is all about deliberate activity, inspired action. Keeping in mind a step is a step. Movement creates clarity.

Communicate- share or exchange info, news or ideas impart or pass on. Synonym- be in touch, interact, meet, talk, speak, converse.

The communicate step for me is all about sharing or exchanging information, ideas, interact, network, touch base.

Celebrate- publicly acknowledge (a significant or happy day or event) with a social gathering or enjoyable activity. Synonyms- commemorate, party, rejoice, glorify

The celebrate step for me is HUGE! We need to make time to celebrate, everyday. I like to dance, color, go for a walk, take a nap, call a friend, sit out back, read a book, listen to music, play a game, take a break, or enjoy my favorite candy bar (just to name a few)

My Daily Clarity- 90 Days to Connect.Create.Communicate.Celebrate

Your Turn

Take a moment and do a braindump for each section. Get it out of your head. Put pen to paper. Now that you know the technical terms for each section what will each section mean to you?

Connect-

_____
_____
_____
_____
_____

Create-

_____
_____
_____
_____
_____

Communicate-

_____
_____
_____
_____
_____

Celebrate-

_____
_____
_____
_____
_____

My Daily Clarity- 90 Days to Connect.Create.Communicate.Celebrate

Why This Book? Why 90 Days?

First, if you're looking for a literary book of genius you've come to the wrong place. I'm just an ordinary woman with simple solutions. I've never claimed to be a writer. I am an exceptional listener, I ask powerful questions, I love to learn and am gifted in communicating and connecting. One of my greatest passions is when I am guiding others on their journey to brilliance.

This book is meant for anyone and anything you want to accomplish in 90 days.

There are several reasons why I chose 90 days. When I was in corporate America, I would hire people and there would be a 90 day grace period for us and them. After 90 days there would be an evaluation and either they could leave or I could ask them to leave. You can see how 90 days was critical to their success.

When I was in direct sales the company I was with had a 90 day success plan. Again, it was set up for our success and along the way if you hit certain milestones you were rewarded. It was proven that most people who completed the 90 day success plan and achieved all the rewards stayed far longer in the company and usually moved into leadership.

Lastly, there's a book that is titled the "12 Week Year: Get More Done in 12 Weeks than Others Do in 12 Months." by Brian P. Moran and Michael Lennington. I found this great synopsis of the book on Amazon.com "This book redefines your "year" to be 12 weeks long. In 12 weeks, there just isn't enough time to get complacent, and urgency increases and intensifies. The 12 Week Year creates focus and clarity on what matters most and a sense of urgency to do it now. In the end more of the important stuff gets done and the impact on results is profound."

My Daily Clarity- 90 Days to Connect.Create.Communicate.Celebrate

Why Accountability?

Back to my good friend google for the technical stuff.

Accountable- (of a person, organization, or institution) required or expected to justify actions or decisions. Synonyms: responsible, answerable.

Have you ever had an accountability partner? Or as we liked to call it within the direct sales company I worked for, a pacing partner?

Several times I enjoyed working with a pacing partner. At one point in my career I worked within a group. We called ourselves the "Limo Ladies". Why? You ask. That's simple, we met in a limo.

We were on an incentive trip in Nashville, TN. A group of us had done so well in earning the trip as a bonus we got a limo ride to Tanya Tucker's house. Needless to say, we hit it off. Before we departed that limo we vowed we would call every week and hold each other accountable in our business and lives.

Following the great success with the limo ladies I connected with a women who would become not only my pacing partner but my soul sister. We took accountability to a new level. We spoke almost every day. My business was never stronger. My family life was incredible. I had someone to not only keep me focused but someone who I could call a life long friend. Our husbands got along, our kids got along, we traveled on incentive trips and for family vacations.

Being accountable to someone works. It feels good. It's fun.

Have no fear, I plan to offer in person and virtual accountability groups. Email me for more information on when and how to join. info@ninaobier.com

My Daily Clarity- 90 Days to Connect.Create.Communicate.Celebrate

You've Got 90 Days- Who will you BE? What will you DO? What will you HAVE? YOU get to choose your FOCUS.

BE
_____
_____
_____
_____
_____

DO
_____
_____
_____
_____
_____

HAVE
_____
_____
_____
_____
_____

90 DAYS TO...
_____
_____
_____
_____
_____

"You have to be before you can do, and do before you can have." Zig Ziglar

My Daily Clarity- 90 Days to Connect.Create.Communicate.Celebrate

"It's All About the J.O.Y.- Journey Of You!"
-Nina Obier

(turn the page and begin)

My Daily Clarity- 90 Days to Connect.Create.Communicate.Celebrate

Let it FLOW!

_____
_____
_____
_____
_____
_____
_____
_____
_____
_____
_____
_____
_____
_____
_____
_____
_____
_____
_____
_____
_____
_____
_____
_____
_____
_____

"When you step into your brilliance
you spark others to step out in theirs" -Nina Obier

My Daily Clarity- 90 Days to Connect.Create.Communicate.Celebrate

My Daily Clarity

Date: _____

Connect — Mind, Body, Spirit

Meditate, Pray, Read, Devotional, Journal, Braindump, Stretch, Exercise, Hydrate, Vision, Mission, Purpose

_____
_____
_____

Create

Deliberate Activity, Plan

_____
_____
_____

Communicate

Share or Exchange Information, Ideas, Interact, Network, Touch Base

_____
_____
_____

Celebrate!

_____
_____
_____

Hydrate

"Clarity is YOUR Currency" -Nina Obier

My Daily Clarity- 90 Days to Connect.Create.Communicate.Celebrate

Let it FLOW!

"When you step into your brilliance
you spark others to step out in theirs" -Nina Obier

My Daily Clarity- 90 Days to Connect.Create.Communicate.Celebrate

My Daily Clarity

Date: _____

Connect — Mind, Body, Spirit
Meditate, Pray, Read, Devotional, Journal, Braindump, Stretch, Exercise, Hydrate, Vision, Mission, Purpose

Create
Deliberate Activity, Plan

Communicate
Share or Exchange Information, Ideas, Interact, Network, Touch Base

Celebrate

Hydrate

"Clarity is YOUR Currency" -Nina Obier

My Daily Clarity- 90 Days to Connect.Create.Communicate.Celebrate

Let it FLOW!

"When you step into your brilliance
you spark others to step out in theirs" -Nina Obier

My Daily Clarity- 90 Days to Connect.Create.Communicate.Celebrate

My Daily Clarity

Date: _____

Connect — Mind, Body, Spirit

Meditate, Pray, Read, Devotional, Journal, Braindump, Stretch, Exercise, Hydrate, Vision, Mission, Purpose

Deliberate Activity, Plan

Create

Communicate — Share or Exchange Information, Ideas, Interact, Network, Touch Base

Celebrate

Hydrate

"Clarity is YOUR Currency" -Nina Obier

My Daily Clarity- 90 Days to Connect.Create.Communicate.Celebrate

Let it FLOW!

"When you step into your brilliance
you spark others to step out in theirs" -Nina Obier

My Daily Clarity- 90 Days to Connect.Create.Communicate.Celebrate

My Daily Clarity

Date: _____

Connect — Mind, Body, Spirit

Meditate, Pray, Read, Devotional, Journal, Braindump, Stretch, Exercise, Hydrate, Vision, Mission, Purpose

_____
_____
_____

Create

Deliberate Activity, Plan

_____
_____
_____

Communicate

Share or Exchange Information, Ideas, Interact, Network, Touch Base

_____
_____
_____

Celebrate

_____
_____
_____

Hydrate

"Clarity is YOUR Currency" -Nina Obier

My Daily Clarity- 90 Days to Connect.Create.Communicate.Celebrate

Let it FLOW!

"When you step into your brilliance
you spark others to step out in theirs" -Nina Obier

My Daily Clarity- 90 Days to Connect.Create.Communicate.Celebrate

My Daily Clarity

Date: _____

Connect — Mind, Body, Spirit

Meditate, Pray, Read, Devotional, Journal, Braindump, Stretch, Exercise, Hydrate, Vision, Mission, Purpose

Create

Deliberate Activity, Plan

Communicate

Share or Exchange Information, Ideas, Interact, Network, Touch Base

Celebrate

Hydrate

"Clarity is YOUR Currency" -Nina Obier

My Daily Clarity- 90 Days to Connect.Create.Communicate.Celebrate

Let it FLOW!

"When you step into your brilliance
you spark others to step out in theirs" -Nina Obier

My Daily Clarity- 90 Days to Connect.Create.Communicate.Celebrate

My Daily Clarity

Date: _____

Connect
- Mind
- Body
- Spirit

Meditate, Pray, Read, Devotional, Journal, Braindump, Stretch, Exercise, Hydrate, Vision, Mission, Purpose

Deliberate Activity, Plan

Create

Communicate

Share or Exchange Information, Ideas, Interact, Network, Touch Base

Celebrate

Hydrate

"Clarity is YOUR Currency" -Nina Obier

My Daily Clarity- 90 Days to Connect.Create.Communicate.Celebrate

Let it FLOW!

Feeling Foggy? Book a Rapid Results Session

"When you step into your brilliance
you spark others to step out in theirs" -Nina Obier

My Daily Clarity- 90 Days to Connect.Create.Communicate.Celebrate

My Daily Clarity

Date: _____

Connect — Mind, Body, Spirit

Meditate, Pray, Read, Devotional, Journal, Braindump, Stretch, Exercise, Hydrate, Vision, Mission, Purpose

Deliberate Activity, Plan

Create

Communicate — Share or Exchange Information, Ideas, Interact, Network, Touch Base

Celebrate

Hydrate

"Clarity is YOUR Currency" -Nina Obier

My Daily Clarity- 90 Days to Connect.Create.Communicate.Celebrate

It's ALL Good!

I give myself a pat on the back for:

_____
_____
_____
_____
_____

I'm feeling so cheerful and blessed:

_____
_____
_____
_____
_____

I say YES to:

_____
_____
_____
_____
_____

Thank you for the clarity on:

_____
_____
_____
_____
_____

"Everyone is trying to accomplish something big, not realizing that life is made up of little things."
-Frank A. Clark

My Daily Clarity- 90 Days to Connect.Create.Communicate.Celebrate

Doodle Page- Color, Mind Map, Imagine, Write Your Favorite Quote/Book/Song/Recipe

My Daily Clarity- 90 Days to Connect.Create.Communicate.Celebrate

Let it FLOW!

___

"When you step into your brilliance
you spark others to step out in theirs" -Nina Obier

My Daily Clarity- 90 Days to Connect.Create.Communicate.Celebrate

My Daily Clarity

Date: _____

Connect — Mind, Body, Spirit

Meditate, Pray, Read, Devotional, Journal, Braindump, Stretch, Exercise, Hydrate, Vision, Mission, Purpose

_____

_____

_____

Create

Deliberate Activity, Plan

_____

_____

_____

Communicate

Share or Exchange Information, Ideas, Interact, Network, Touch Base

_____

_____

_____

Celebrate

_____

_____

_____

Hydrate

"Clarity is YOUR Currency" -Nina Obier

My Daily Clarity- 90 Days to Connect.Create.Communicate.Celebrate

Let it FLOW!

___

"When you step into your brilliance
you spark others to step out in theirs" -Nina Obier

My Daily Clarity- 90 Days to Connect.Create.Communicate.Celebrate

My Daily Clarity

Date: _____

Connect — Mind, Body, Spirit

Meditate, Pray, Read, Devotional, Journal, Braindump, Stretch, Exercise, Hydrate, Vision, Mission, Purpose

Create

Deliberate Activity, Plan

Communicate

Share or Exchange Information, Ideas, Interact, Network, Touch Base

Celebrate

Hydrate

"Clarity is YOUR Currency" -Nina Obier

My Daily Clarity- 90 Days to Connect.Create.Communicate.Celebrate

Let it FLOW!

"When you step into your brilliance
you spark others to step out in theirs" -Nina Obier

My Daily Clarity- 90 Days to Connect.Create.Communicate.Celebrate

My Daily Clarity

Date: _____

Connect — Mind, Body, Spirit

Meditate, Pray, Read, Devotional, Journal, Braindump, Stretch, Exercise, Hydrate, Vision, Mission, Purpose

Create — Deliberate Activity, Plan

Communicate — Share or Exchange Information, Ideas, Interact, Network, Touch Base

Celebrate

Hydrate

"Clarity is YOUR Currency" -Nina Obier

My Daily Clarity- 90 Days to Connect.Create.Communicate.Celebrate

Let it FLOW!

"When you step into your brilliance
you spark others to step out in theirs" -Nina Obier

My Daily Clarity- 90 Days to Connect.Create.Communicate.Celebrate

My Daily Clarity

Date: _____

Connect — Mind, Body, Spirit

Meditate, Pray, Read, Devotional, Journal, Braindump, Stretch, Exercise, Hydrate, Vision, Mission, Purpose

Create

Deliberate Activity, Plan

Communicate

Share or Exchange Information, Ideas, Interact, Network, Touch Base

Celebrate

Hydrate

"Clarity is YOUR Currency" -Nina Obier

My Daily Clarity- 90 Days to Connect.Create.Communicate.Celebrate

Let it FLOW!

"When you step into your brilliance
you spark others to step out in theirs" -Nina Obier

My Daily Clarity- 90 Days to Connect.Create.Communicate.Celebrate

My Daily Clarity

Date: _____

Connect — Mind, Body, Spirit

Meditate, Pray, Read, Devotional, Journal, Braindump, Stretch, Exercise, Hydrate, Vision, Mission, Purpose

_____
_____
_____

Create

Deliberate Activity, Plan

_____
_____
_____

Communicate

Share or Exchange Information, Ideas, Interact, Network, Touch Base

_____
_____
_____

Celebrate

_____
_____
_____

Hydrate

"Clarity is YOUR Currency" -Nina Obier

My Daily Clarity- 90 Days to Connect.Create.Communicate.Celebrate

Let it FLOW!

_____

"When you step into your brilliance
you spark others to step out in theirs" -Nina Obier

My Daily Clarity- 90 Days to Connect.Create.Communicate.Celebrate

My Daily Clarity

Date: _____

Connect
- Mind
- Body
- Spirit

Meditate, Pray, Read, Devotional, Journal, Braindump, Stretch, Exercise, Hydrate, Vision, Mission, Purpose

Create

Deliberate Activity, Plan

Communicate

Share or Exchange Information, Ideas, Interact, Network, Touch Base

Celebrate

Hydrate

"Clarity is YOUR Currency" -Nina Obier

My Daily Clarity- 90 Days to Connect.Create.Communicate.Celebrate

Let it FLOW!

Need Clarity? Book a Rapid Results Session

"When you step into your brilliance
you spark others to step out in theirs" -Nina Obier

My Daily Clarity- 90 Days to Connect.Create.Communicate.Celebrate

My Daily Clarity

Date: _____

Connect — Mind, Body, Spirit
Meditate, Pray, Read, Devotional, Journal, Braindump, Stretch, Exercise, Hydrate, Vision, Mission, Purpose

_____
_____
_____

Create
Deliberate Activity, Plan

_____
_____

Communicate
Share or Exchange Information, Ideas, Interact, Network, Touch Base

_____
_____
_____

Celebrate

_____
_____
_____

Hydrate

"Clarity is YOUR Currency" -Nina Obier

My Daily Clarity- 90 Days to Connect.Create.Communicate.Celebrate

It's ALL Good!

I give myself a pat on the back for:

_____
_____
_____
_____
_____

I'm feeling so cheerful and blessed:

_____
_____
_____
_____
_____

I say YES to:

_____
_____
_____
_____
_____

Thank you for the clarity on:

_____
_____
_____
_____

"Efficiency is doing things right. Effectiveness is doing the right thing." -Alan Nelson

My Daily Clarity- 90 Days to Connect.Create.Communicate.Celebrate

Doodle Page- Color, Mind Map, Imagine, Write Your Favorite Quote/Book/Song/Recipe

My Daily Clarity- 90 Days to Connect.Create.Communicate.Celebrate

Let it FLOW!

___

"When you step into your brilliance
you spark others to step out in theirs" -Nina Obier

My Daily Clarity- 90 Days to Connect.Create.Communicate.Celebrate

My Daily Clarity

Date: _____

Connect
Mind
Body
Spirit

Meditate, Pray, Read, Devotional, Journal, Braindump, Stretch, Exercise, Hydrate, Vision, Mission, Purpose

Deliberate Activity, Plan

Create

Communicate

Share or Exchange Information, Ideas, Interact, Network, Touch Base

Celebrate

Hydrate

"Clarity is YOUR Currency" -Nina Obier

My Daily Clarity- 90 Days to Connect.Create.Communicate.Celebrate

Let it FLOW!

"When you step into your brilliance
you spark others to step out in theirs" -Nina Obier

My Daily Clarity- 90 Days to Connect.Create.Communicate.Celebrate

My Daily Clarity

Date: _____

Connect — Mind, Body, Spirit

Meditate, Pray, Read, Devotional, Journal, Braindump, Stretch, Exercise, Hydrate, Vision, Mission, Purpose

_____
_____
_____
_____

Create

Deliberate Activity, Plan

_____
_____
_____

Communicate

Share or Exchange Information, Ideas, Interact, Network, Touch Base

_____
_____
_____

Celebrate

_____
_____
_____

Hydrate

"Clarity is YOUR Currency" -Nina Obier

My Daily Clarity- 90 Days to Connect.Create.Communicate.Celebrate

Let it FLOW!

"When you step into your brilliance
you spark others to step out in theirs" -Nina Obier

My Daily Clarity- 90 Days to Connect.Create.Communicate.Celebrate

My Daily Clarity

Date: _____

Connect
- Mind
- Body
- Spirit

Meditate, Pray, Read, Devotional, Journal, Braindump, Stretch, Exercise, Hydrate, Vision, Mission, Purpose

Create

Deliberate Activity, Plan

Communicate

Share or Exchange Information, Ideas, Interact, Network, Touch Base

Celebrate

Hydrate

"Clarity is YOUR Currency" -Nina Obier

My Daily Clarity- 90 Days to Connect.Create.Communicate.Celebrate

Let it FLOW!

___

"When you step into your brilliance
you spark others to step out in theirs" -Nina Obier

My Daily Clarity- 90 Days to Connect.Create.Communicate.Celebrate

My Daily Clarity

Date: _____

Connect — Mind, Body, Spirit
Meditate, Pray, Read, Devotional, Journal, Braindump, Stretch, Exercise, Hydrate, Vision, Mission, Purpose

Create
Deliberate Activity, Plan

Communicate
Share or Exchange Information, Ideas, Interact, Network, Touch Base

Celebrate

Hydrate

"Clarity is YOUR Currency" -Nina Obier

My Daily Clarity- 90 Days to Connect.Create.Communicate.Celebrate

Let it FLOW!

"When you step into your brilliance
you spark others to step out in theirs" -Nina Obier

My Daily Clarity- 90 Days to Connect.Create.Communicate.Celebrate

My Daily Clarity   Date: _____

Connect — Mind, Body, Spirit

Meditate, Pray, Read, Devotional, Journal, Braindump, Stretch, Exercise, Hydrate, Vision, Mission, Purpose

_____

_____

_____

Create

Deliberate Activity, Plan

_____

_____

Communicate

Share or Exchange Information, Ideas, Interact, Network, Touch Base

_____

_____

_____

Celebrate

_____

_____

_____

Hydrate

"Clarity is YOUR Currency" -Nina Obier

My Daily Clarity- 90 Days to Connect.Create.Communicate.Celebrate

Let it FLOW!

"When you step into your brilliance
you spark others to step out in theirs" -Nina Obier

My Daily Clarity- 90 Days to Connect.Create.Communicate.Celebrate

My Daily Clarity

Date: _____

Connect — Mind, Body, Spirit

Meditate, Pray, Read, Devotional, Journal, Braindump, Stretch, Exercise, Hydrate, Vision, Mission, Purpose

_____
_____
_____
_____

Create

Deliberate Activity, Plan

_____
_____

Communicate

Share or Exchange Information, Ideas, Interact, Network, Touch Base

_____
_____
_____

Celebrate

_____
_____
_____

Hydrate (8 glasses)

"Clarity is YOUR Currency" -Nina Obier

My Daily Clarity- 90 Days to Connect.Create.Communicate.Celebrate

Let it FLOW!

Feeling Stuck? Book Rapid Results Session

"When you step into your brilliance
you spark others to step out in theirs" -Nina Obier

My Daily Clarity- 90 Days to Connect.Create.Communicate.Celebrate

My Daily Clarity

Date: _____

Connect
- Mind
- Body
- Spirit

Meditate, Pray, Read, Devotional, Journal, Braindump, Stretch, Exercise, Hydrate, Vision, Mission, Purpose

_____
_____
_____

Create

Deliberate Activity, Plan

_____
_____
_____

Communicate

Share or Exchange Information, Ideas, Interact, Network, Touch Base

_____
_____
_____

Celebrate

_____
_____
_____

Hydrate

"Clarity is YOUR Currency" -Nina Obier

My Daily Clarity- 90 Days to Connect.Create.Communicate.Celebrate

It's ALL Good!

I give myself a pat on the back for:

_____
_____
_____
_____
_____

I'm feeling so cheerful and blessed:

_____
_____
_____
_____
_____

I say YES to:

_____
_____
_____
_____
_____

Thank you for the clarity on:

_____
_____
_____
_____
_____

"Either you run the day or the day runs you."
-J. C. McPheeters

My Daily Clarity- 90 Days to Connect.Create.Communicate.Celebrate

Doodle Page- Color, Mind Map, Imagine, Write Your Favorite Quote/Book/Song/Recipe

My Daily Clarity- 90 Days to Connect.Create.Communicate.Celebrate

Let it FLOW!

"When you step into your brilliance
you spark others to step out in theirs" -Nina Obier

My Daily Clarity- 90 Days to Connect.Create.Communicate.Celebrate

My Daily Clarity

Date: _____

Connect
Mind
Body
Spirit

Meditate, Pray, Read, Devotional, Journal, Braindump, Stretch, Exercise, Hydrate, Vision, Mission, Purpose

Deliberate Activity, Plan

Create

Communicate

Share or Exchange Information, Ideas, Interact, Network, Touch Base

Celebrate

Hydrate

"Clarity is YOUR Currency" -Nina Obier

My Daily Clarity- 90 Days to Connect.Create.Communicate.Celebrate

Let it FLOW!

"When you step into your brilliance
you spark others to step out in theirs" -Nina Obier

My Daily Clarity- 90 Days to Connect.Create.Communicate.Celebrate

My Daily Clarity

Date: _____

Connect — Mind, Body, Spirit

Meditate, Pray, Read, Devotional, Journal, Braindump, Stretch, Exercise, Hydrate, Vision, Mission, Purpose

_____
_____
_____
_____

Create

Deliberate Activity, Plan

_____
_____

Communicate

Share or Exchange Information, Ideas, Interact, Network, Touch Base

_____
_____
_____

Celebrate

_____
_____

Hydrate

"Clarity is YOUR Currency" -Nina Obier

My Daily Clarity- 90 Days to Connect.Create.Communicate.Celebrate

Let it FLOW!

"When you step into your brilliance you spark others to step out in theirs" -Nina Obier

My Daily Clarity- 90 Days to Connect.Create.Communicate.Celebrate

My Daily Clarity

Date: _____

Connect — Mind, Body, Spirit

Meditate, Pray, Read, Devotional, Journal, Braindump, Stretch, Exercise, Hydrate, Vision, Mission, Purpose

_____

_____

_____

Create

Deliberate Activity, Plan

_____

_____

Communicate

Share or Exchange Information, Ideas, Interact, Network, Touch Base

_____

_____

_____

Celebrate

_____

_____

_____

"Clarity is YOUR Currency" -Nina Obier

Hydrate

My Daily Clarity- 90 Days to Connect.Create.Communicate.Celebrate

Let it FLOW!

___

"When you step into your brilliance
you spark others to step out in theirs" -Nina Obier

My Daily Clarity- 90 Days to Connect.Create.Communicate.Celebrate

My Daily Clarity

Date: _____

Connect — Mind, Body, Spirit

Meditate, Pray, Read, Devotional, Journal, Braindump, Stretch, Exercise, Hydrate, Vision, Mission, Purpose

_____
_____
_____

Deliberate Activity, Plan

Create

_____
_____
_____

Communicate

Share or Exchange Information, Ideas, Interact, Network, Touch Base

_____
_____
_____

Celebrate

_____
_____
_____

Hydrate

"Clarity is YOUR Currency" -Nina Obier

My Daily Clarity- 90 Days to Connect.Create.Communicate.Celebrate

Let it FLOW!

"When you step into your brilliance
you spark others to step out in theirs" -Nina Obier

My Daily Clarity- 90 Days to Connect.Create.Communicate.Celebrate

My Daily Clarity

Date: _____

Connect
- Mind
- Body
- Spirit

Meditate, Pray, Read, Devotional, Journal, Braindump, Stretch, Exercise, Hydrate, Vision, Mission, Purpose

Create
Deliberate Activity, Plan

Communicate
Share or Exchange Information, Ideas, Interact, Network, Touch Base

Celebrate

Hydrate

"Clarity is YOUR Currency" -Nina Obier

My Daily Clarity- 90 Days to Connect.Create.Communicate.Celebrate

Let it FLOW!

"When you step into your brilliance
you spark others to step out in theirs" -Nina Obier

My Daily Clarity- 90 Days to Connect.Create.Communicate.Celebrate

My Daily Clarity

Date: _____

Connect — Mind, Body, Spirit

Meditate, Pray, Read, Devotional, Journal, Braindump, Stretch, Exercise, Hydrate, Vision, Mission, Purpose

_____
_____
_____

Create — Deliberate Activity, Plan

_____
_____
_____

Communicate — Share or Exchange Information, Ideas, Interact, Network, Touch Base

_____
_____
_____

Celebrate

_____
_____
_____

Hydrate

"Clarity is YOUR Currency" -Nina Obier

My Daily Clarity- 90 Days to Connect.Create.Communicate.Celebrate

Let it FLOW!

Ready For More? Book a Rapid Results Session

"When you step into your brilliance
you spark others to step out in theirs" -Nina Obier

My Daily Clarity- 90 Days to Connect.Create.Communicate.Celebrate

My Daily Clarity

Date: _____

Connect
- Mind
- Body
- Spirit

Meditate, Pray, Read, Devotional, Journal, Braindump, Stretch, Exercise, Hydrate, Vision, Mission, Purpose

Create
Deliberate Activity, Plan

Communicate
Share or Exchange Information, Ideas, Interact, Network, Touch Base

Celebrate

Hydrate

"Clarity is YOUR Currency" -Nina Obier

My Daily Clarity- 90 Days to Connect.Create.Communicate.Celebrate

It's ALL Good!

I give myself a pat on the back for:
_____
_____
_____
_____
_____

I'm feeling so cheerful and blessed:
_____
_____
_____
_____
_____

I say YES to:
_____
_____
_____
_____
_____

Thank you for the clarity on:
_____
_____
_____
_____

"Imagination is the beginning of creativity."
-George Bernard Shaw

My Daily Clarity- 90 Days to Connect.Create.Communicate.Celebrate

Doodle Page- Color, Mind Map, Imagine, Write Your Favorite Quote/Book/Song/Recipe

My Daily Clarity- 90 Days to Connect.Create.Communicate.Celebrate

Let it FLOW!

"When you step into your brilliance
you spark others to step out in theirs" -Nina Obier

My Daily Clarity- 90 Days to Connect.Create.Communicate.Celebrate

My Daily Clarity

Date: _____

Connect — Mind, Body, Spirit

Meditate, Pray, Read, Devotional, Journal, Braindump, Stretch, Exercise, Hydrate, Vision, Mission, Purpose

Create

Deliberate Activity, Plan

Communicate

Share or Exchange Information, Ideas, Interact, Network, Touch Base

Celebrate

Hydrate

"Clarity is YOUR Currency" -Nina Obier

My Daily Clarity- 90 Days to Connect.Create.Communicate.Celebrate

Let it FLOW!

"When you step into your brilliance
you spark others to step out in theirs" -Nina Obier

My Daily Clarity- 90 Days to Connect.Create.Communicate.Celebrate

My Daily Clarity

Date: _____

Connect — Mind, Body, Spirit

Meditate, Pray, Read, Devotional, Journal, Braindump, Stretch, Exercise, Hydrate, Vision, Mission, Purpose

Create

Deliberate Activity, Plan

Communicate

Share or Exchange Information, Ideas, Interact, Network, Touch Base

Celebrate

Hydrate

"Clarity is YOUR Currency" -Nina Obier

My Daily Clarity- 90 Days to Connect.Create.Communicate.Celebrate

Let it FLOW!

"When you step into your brilliance
you spark others to step out in theirs" -Nina Obier

My Daily Clarity- 90 Days to Connect.Create.Communicate.Celebrate

My Daily Clarity

Date: _____

Connect — Mind, Body, Spirit
Meditate, Pray, Read, Devotional, Journal, Braindump, Stretch, Exercise, Hydrate, Vision, Mission, Purpose

Create
Deliberate Activity, Plan

Communicate
Share or Exchange Information, Ideas, Interact, Network, Touch Base

Celebrate

Hydrate

"Clarity is YOUR Currency" -Nina Obier

My Daily Clarity- 90 Days to Connect.Create.Communicate.Celebrate

Let it FLOW!

"When you step into your brilliance
you spark others to step out in theirs" -Nina Obier

My Daily Clarity- 90 Days to Connect.Create.Communicate.Celebrate

My Daily Clarity   Date: _____

Connect — Mind, Body, Spirit

Meditate, Pray, Read, Devotional, Journal, Braindump, Stretch, Exercise, Hydrate, Vision, Mission, Purpose

Create

Deliberate Activity, Plan

Communicate

Share or Exchange Information, Ideas, Interact, Network, Touch Base

Celebrate

Hydrate

"Clarity is YOUR Currency" -Nina Obier

My Daily Clarity- 90 Days to Connect.Create.Communicate.Celebrate

Let it FLOW!

_____

"When you step into your brilliance
you spark others to step out in theirs" -Nina Obier

My Daily Clarity- 90 Days to Connect.Create.Communicate.Celebrate

My Daily Clarity   Date: _____

Connect — Mind, Body, Spirit

Meditate, Pray, Read, Devotional, Journal, Braindump, Stretch, Exercise, Hydrate, Vision, Mission, Purpose

_____
_____
_____

Create — Deliberate Activity, Plan

_____
_____
_____

Communicate — Share or Exchange Information, Ideas, Interact, Network, Touch Base

_____
_____
_____

Celebrate

_____
_____

Hydrate

"Clarity is YOUR Currency" -Nina Obier

My Daily Clarity- 90 Days to Connect.Create.Communicate.Celebrate

Let it FLOW!

Feeling Foggy? Book a Rapid Results Session

"When you step into your brilliance
you spark others to step out in theirs" -Nina Obier

My Daily Clarity- 90 Days to Connect.Create.Communicate.Celebrate

My Daily Clarity

Date: _____

Connect — Mind, Body, Spirit

Meditate, Pray, Read, Devotional, Journal, Braindump, Stretch, Exercise, Hydrate, Vision, Mission, Purpose

Create

Deliberate Activity, Plan

Communicate

Share or Exchange Information, Ideas, Interact, Network, Touch Base

Celebrate

Hydrate

"Clarity is YOUR Currency" -Nina Obier

My Daily Clarity- 90 Days to Connect.Create.Communicate.Celebrate

It's ALL Good!

I give myself a pat on the back for:
_____
_____
_____
_____
_____

I'm feeling so cheerful and blessed:
_____
_____
_____
_____
_____

I say YES to:
_____
_____
_____
_____
_____

Thank you for the clarity on:
_____
_____
_____
_____

"The first step to wisdom is silence; the second is listening." -Carl Summer

My Daily Clarity- 90 Days to Connect.Create.Communicate.Celebrate

Doodle Page- Color, Mind Map, Imagine, Write Your Favorite Quote/Book/Song/Recipe

My Daily Clarity- 90 Days to Connect.Create.Communicate.Celebrate

Let it FLOW!

"When you step into your brilliance
you spark others to step out in theirs" -Nina Obier

My Daily Clarity- 90 Days to Connect.Create.Communicate.Celebrate

My Daily Clarity

Date: _____

Connect — Mind, Body, Spirit

Meditate, Pray, Read, Devotional, Journal, Braindump, Stretch, Exercise, Hydrate, Vision, Mission, Purpose

_____
_____
_____

Create

Deliberate Activity, Plan

_____
_____
_____

Communicate

Share or Exchange Information, Ideas, Interact, Network, Touch Base

_____
_____
_____

Celebrate

_____
_____
_____

Hydrate

"Clarity is YOUR Currency" -Nina Obier

My Daily Clarity- 90 Days to Connect.Create.Communicate.Celebrate

Let it FLOW!

"When you step into your brilliance
you spark others to step out in theirs" -Nina Obier

My Daily Clarity- 90 Days to Connect.Create.Communicate.Celebrate

My Daily Clarity

Date: _____

Connect — Mind, Body, Spirit

Meditate, Pray, Read, Devotional, Journal, Braindump, Stretch, Exercise, Hydrate, Vision, Mission, Purpose

_____
_____
_____
_____
_____
_____

Create

Deliberate Activity, Plan

_____
_____
_____

Communicate

Share or Exchange Information, Ideas, Interact, Network, Touch Base

_____
_____
_____

Celebrate

_____
_____
_____

Hydrate

"Clarity is YOUR Currency" -Nina Obier

My Daily Clarity- 90 Days to Connect.Create.Communicate.Celebrate

Let it FLOW!

"When you step into your brilliance
you spark others to step out in theirs" -Nina Obier

My Daily Clarity- 90 Days to Connect.Create.Communicate.Celebrate

My Daily Clarity

Date: _____

Connect — Mind, Body, Spirit

Meditate, Pray, Read, Devotional, Journal, Braindump, Stretch, Exercise, Hydrate, Vision, Mission, Purpose

Create

Deliberate Activity, Plan

Communicate

Share or Exchange Information, Ideas, Interact, Network, Touch Base

Celebrate

Hydrate

"Clarity is YOUR Currency" -Nina Obier

My Daily Clarity- 90 Days to Connect.Create.Communicate.Celebrate

Let it FLOW!

"When you step into your brilliance
you spark others to step out in theirs" -Nina Obier

My Daily Clarity- 90 Days to Connect.Create.Communicate.Celebrate

My Daily Clarity

Date: _____

Connect — Mind, Body, Spirit

Meditate, Pray, Read, Devotional, Journal, Braindump, Stretch, Exercise, Hydrate, Vision, Mission, Purpose

Create

Deliberate Activity, Plan

Communicate

Share or Exchange Information, Ideas, Interact, Network, Touch Base

Celebrate

Hydrate

"Clarity is YOUR Currency" -Nina Obier

My Daily Clarity- 90 Days to Connect.Create.Communicate.Celebrate

Let it FLOW!

"When you step into your brilliance
you spark others to step out in theirs" -Nina Obier

My Daily Clarity- 90 Days to Connect.Create.Communicate.Celebrate

My Daily Clarity

Date: _____

Connect
- Mind
- Body
- Spirit

Meditate, Pray, Read, Devotional, Journal, Braindump, Stretch, Exercise, Hydrate, Vision, Mission, Purpose

Create
Deliberate Activity, Plan

Communicate
Share or Exchange Information, Ideas, Interact, Network, Touch Base

Celebrate

Hydrate

"Clarity is YOUR Currency" -Nina Obier

My Daily Clarity- 90 Days to Connect.Create.Communicate.Celebrate

Let it FLOW!

"When you step into your brilliance
you spark others to step out in theirs" -Nina Obier

My Daily Clarity- 90 Days to Connect.Create.Communicate.Celebrate

My Daily Clarity

Date: _____

Connect — Mind, Body, Spirit

Meditate, Pray, Read, Devotional, Journal, Braindump, Stretch, Exercise, Hydrate, Vision, Mission, Purpose

Create

Deliberate Activity, Plan

Communicate

Share or Exchange Information, Ideas, Interact, Network, Touch Base

Celebrate

Hydrate

"Clarity is YOUR Currency" -Nina Obier

My Daily Clarity- 90 Days to Connect.Create.Communicate.Celebrate

Let it FLOW!

Need Clarity? Book a Rapid Results Session

"When you step into your brilliance
you spark others to step out in theirs" -Nina Obier

My Daily Clarity- 90 Days to Connect.Create.Communicate.Celebrate

My Daily Clarity

Date: _____

Connect — Mind, Body, Spirit

Meditate, Pray, Read, Devotional, Journal, Braindump, Stretch, Exercise, Hydrate, Vision, Mission, Purpose

Create

Deliberate Activity, Plan

Communicate

Share or Exchange Information, Ideas, Interact, Network, Touch Base

Celebrate

Hydrate

"Clarity is YOUR Currency" -Nina Obier

My Daily Clarity- 90 Days to Connect.Create.Communicate.Celebrate

It's ALL Good!

I give myself a pat on the back for:

_____
_____
_____
_____
_____

I'm feeling so cheerful and blessed:

_____
_____
_____
_____
_____

I say YES to:

_____
_____
_____
_____
_____

Thank you for the clarity on:

_____
_____
_____
_____

**"Take action out of inspiration, not desperation."
-Unknown**

My Daily Clarity- 90 Days to Connect.Create.Communicate.Celebrate

Doodle Page- Color, Mind Map, Imagine, Write Your Favorite Quote/Book/Song/Recipe

My Daily Clarity- 90 Days to Connect.Create.Communicate.Celebrate

Let it FLOW!

"When you step into your brilliance
you spark others to step out in theirs" -Nina Obier

My Daily Clarity- 90 Days to Connect.Create.Communicate.Celebrate

My Daily Clarity

Date: _____

Connect
- Mind
- Body
- Spirit

Meditate, Pray, Read, Devotional, Journal, Braindump, Stretch, Exercise, Hydrate, Vision, Mission, Purpose

Create
Deliberate Activity, Plan

Communicate
Share or Exchange Information, Ideas, Interact, Network, Touch Base

Celebrate

Hydrate

"Clarity is YOUR Currency" -Nina Obier

Let it FLOW!

"When you step into your brilliance
you spark others to step out in theirs" -Nina Obier

My Daily Clarity- 90 Days to Connect.Create.Communicate.Celebrate

My Daily Clarity

Date: _____

Connect — Mind, Body, Spirit

Meditate, Pray, Read, Devotional, Journal, Braindump, Stretch, Exercise, Hydrate, Vision, Mission, Purpose

Create

Deliberate Activity, Plan

Communicate

Share or Exchange Information, Ideas, Interact, Network, Touch Base

Celebrate

Hydrate

"Clarity is YOUR Currency" -Nina Obier

My Daily Clarity- 90 Days to Connect.Create.Communicate.Celebrate

Let it FLOW!

"When you step into your brilliance
you spark others to step out in theirs" -Nina Obier

My Daily Clarity- 90 Days to Connect.Create.Communicate.Celebrate

My Daily Clarity

Date: _____

Connect — Mind, Body, Spirit

Meditate, Pray, Read, Devotional, Journal, Braindump, Stretch, Exercise, Hydrate, Vision, Mission, Purpose

Create

Deliberate Activity, Plan

Communicate

Share or Exchange Information, Ideas, Interact, Network, Touch Base

Celebrate

Hydrate

"Clarity is YOUR Currency" -Nina Obier

My Daily Clarity- 90 Days to Connect.Create.Communicate.Celebrate

Let it FLOW!

"When you step into your brilliance you spark others to step out in theirs" -Nina Obier

My Daily Clarity- 90 Days to Connect.Create.Communicate.Celebrate

My Daily Clarity

Date: _____

Connect — Mind, Body, Spirit

Meditate, Pray, Read, Devotional, Journal, Braindump, Stretch, Exercise, Hydrate, Vision, Mission, Purpose

Deliberate Activity, Plan

Create

Communicate — Share or Exchange Information, Ideas, Interact, Network, Touch Base

Celebrate

Hydrate

"Clarity is YOUR Currency" -Nina Obier

My Daily Clarity- 90 Days to Connect.Create.Communicate.Celebrate

Let it FLOW!

_____

"When you step into your brilliance
you spark others to step out in theirs" -Nina Obier

My Daily Clarity- 90 Days to Connect.Create.Communicate.Celebrate

My Daily Clarity

Date: _____

Connect
- Mind
- Body
- Spirit

Meditate, Pray, Read, Devotional, Journal, Braindump, Stretch, Exercise, Hydrate, Vision, Mission, Purpose

Deliberate Activity, Plan

Create

Communicate

Share or Exchange Information, Ideas, Interact, Network, Touch Base

Celebrate

Hydrate

"Clarity is YOUR Currency" -Nina Obier

My Daily Clarity- 90 Days to Connect.Create.Communicate.Celebrate

Let it FLOW!

_____

"When you step into your brilliance
you spark others to step out in theirs" -Nina Obier

My Daily Clarity- 90 Days to Connect.Create.Communicate.Celebrate

My Daily Clarity

Date: _____

Connect — Mind, Body, Spirit

Meditate, Pray, Read, Devotional, Journal, Braindump, Stretch, Exercise, Hydrate, Vision, Mission, Purpose

Create

Deliberate Activity, Plan

Communicate

Share or Exchange Information, Ideas, Interact, Network, Touch Base

Celebrate

Hydrate

"Clarity is YOUR Currency" -Nina Obier

My Daily Clarity- 90 Days to Connect.Create.Communicate.Celebrate

Let it FLOW!

Feeling Stuck? Book a Rapid Results Session

"When you step into your brilliance
you spark others to step out in theirs" -Nina Obier

My Daily Clarity- 90 Days to Connect.Create.Communicate.Celebrate

My Daily Clarity

Date: _____

Connect — Mind, Body, Spirit

Meditate, Pray, Read, Devotional, Journal, Braindump, Stretch, Exercise, Hydrate, Vision, Mission, Purpose

Create

Deliberate Activity, Plan

Communicate

Share or Exchange Information, Ideas, Interact, Network, Touch Base

Celebrate

Hydrate

"Clarity is YOUR Currency" -Nina Obier

My Daily Clarity- 90 Days to Connect.Create.Communicate.Celebrate

It's ALL Good!

I give myself a pat on the back for:

_____
_____
_____
_____
_____

I'm feeling so cheerful and blessed:

_____
_____
_____
_____
_____

I say YES to:

_____
_____
_____
_____
_____

Thank you for the clarity on:

_____
_____
_____
_____

"We can do anything we want as long as we stick to it." -Helen Keller

My Daily Clarity- 90 Days to Connect.Create.Communicate.Celebrate

Doodle Page- Color, Mind Map, Imagine, Write Your Favorite Quote/Book/Song/Recipe

My Daily Clarity- 90 Days to Connect.Create.Communicate.Celebrate

Let it FLOW!

"When you step into your brilliance
you spark others to step out in theirs" -Nina Obier

My Daily Clarity- 90 Days to Connect.Create.Communicate.Celebrate

My Daily Clarity

Date: _____

Connect — Mind, Body, Spirit

Meditate, Pray, Read, Devotional, Journal, Braindump, Stretch, Exercise, Hydrate, Vision, Mission, Purpose

_____
_____
_____

Create

Deliberate Activity, Plan

_____
_____
_____

Communicate

Share or Exchange Information, Ideas, Interact, Network, Touch Base

_____
_____
_____

Celebrate

_____
_____
_____

Hydrate

"Clarity is YOUR Currency" -Nina Obier

My Daily Clarity- 90 Days to Connect.Create.Communicate.Celebrate

Let it FLOW!

"When you step into your brilliance
you spark others to step out in theirs" -Nina Obier

My Daily Clarity- 90 Days to Connect.Create.Communicate.Celebrate

My Daily Clarity

Date: _____

Connect — Mind, Body, Spirit

Meditate, Pray, Read, Devotional, Journal, Braindump, Stretch, Exercise, Hydrate, Vision, Mission, Purpose

Create

Deliberate Activity, Plan

Communicate

Share or Exchange Information, Ideas, Interact, Network, Touch Base

Celebrate

Hydrate

"Clarity is YOUR Currency" -Nina Obier

My Daily Clarity- 90 Days to Connect.Create.Communicate.Celebrate

Let it FLOW!

"When you step into your brilliance
you spark others to step out in theirs" -Nina Obier

My Daily Clarity- 90 Days to Connect.Create.Communicate.Celebrate

My Daily Clarity

Date: _____

Connect — Mind, Body, Spirit
Meditate, Pray, Read, Devotional, Journal, Braindump, Stretch, Exercise, Hydrate, Vision, Mission, Purpose

Create
Deliberate Activity, Plan

Communicate
Share or Exchange Information, Ideas, Interact, Network, Touch Base

Celebrate

Hydrate

"Clarity is YOUR Currency" -Nina Obier

My Daily Clarity- 90 Days to Connect.Create.Communicate.Celebrate

Let it FLOW!

"When you step into your brilliance
you spark others to step out in theirs" -Nina Obier

My Daily Clarity- 90 Days to Connect.Create.Communicate.Celebrate

My Daily Clarity

Date: _____

Connect — Mind, Body, Spirit

Meditate, Pray, Read, Devotional, Journal, Braindump, Stretch, Exercise, Hydrate, Vision, Mission, Purpose

_____
_____
_____

Create

Deliberate Activity, Plan

_____
_____
_____

Communicate

Share or Exchange Information, Ideas, Interact, Network, Touch Base

_____
_____
_____

Celebrate

_____
_____
_____

Hydrate

"Clarity is YOUR Currency" -Nina Obier

My Daily Clarity- 90 Days to Connect.Create.Communicate.Celebrate

Let it FLOW!

"When you step into your brilliance
you spark others to step out in theirs" -Nina Obier

My Daily Clarity- 90 Days to Connect.Create.Communicate.Celebrate

My Daily Clarity

Date: _____

Connect — Mind, Body, Spirit

Meditate, Pray, Read, Devotional, Journal, Braindump, Stretch, Exercise, Hydrate, Vision, Mission, Purpose

Create

Deliberate Activity, Plan

Communicate

Share or Exchange Information, Ideas, Interact, Network, Touch Base

Celebrate

Hydrate

"Clarity is YOUR Currency" -Nina Obier

My Daily Clarity- 90 Days to Connect.Create.Communicate.Celebrate

Let it FLOW!

"When you step into your brilliance you spark others to step out in theirs" -Nina Obier

My Daily Clarity- 90 Days to Connect.Create.Communicate.Celebrate

My Daily Clarity

Date: _____

Connect — Mind, Body, Spirit

Meditate, Pray, Read, Devotional, Journal, Braindump, Stretch, Exercise, Hydrate, Vision, Mission, Purpose

Create

Deliberate Activity, Plan

Communicate

Share or Exchange Information, Ideas, Interact, Network, Touch Base

Celebrate

Hydrate

"Clarity is YOUR Currency" -Nina Obier

My Daily Clarity- 90 Days to Connect.Create.Communicate.Celebrate

Let it FLOW!

Ready For More? Book Rapid Results Session

"When you step into your brilliance
you spark others to step out in theirs" -Nina Obier

My Daily Clarity- 90 Days to Connect.Create.Communicate.Celebrate

My Daily Clarity

Date: _____

Connect
- Mind
- Body
- Spirit

Meditate, Pray, Read, Devotional, Journal, Braindump, Stretch, Exercise, Hydrate, Vision, Mission, Purpose

_____
_____
_____

Create

Deliberate Activity, Plan

_____
_____
_____

Communicate

Share or Exchange Information, Ideas, Interact, Network, Touch Base

_____
_____
_____

Celebrate

_____
_____
_____

Hydrate

"Clarity is YOUR Currency" -Nina Obier

My Daily Clarity- 90 Days to Connect.Create.Communicate.Celebrate

It's ALL Good!

I give myself a pat on the back for:

_____
_____
_____
_____
_____

I'm feeling so cheerful and blessed:

_____
_____
_____
_____
_____

I say YES to:

_____
_____
_____
_____
_____

Thank you for the clarity on:

_____
_____
_____
_____
_____

"Celebrate the happiness that friends are always giving, make every day a holiday and celebrate just living." -Amanda Bradley

My Daily Clarity- 90 Days to Connect.Create.Communicate.Celebrate

Doodle Page- Color, Mind Map, Imagine, Write Your Favorite Quote/Book/Song/Recipe

My Daily Clarity- 90 Days to Connect.Create.Communicate.Celebrate

Let it FLOW!

_____

"When you step into your brilliance
you spark others to step out in theirs" -Nina Obier

My Daily Clarity- 90 Days to Connect.Create.Communicate.Celebrate

My Daily Clarity

Date: _____

Connect — Mind, Body, Spirit

Meditate, Pray, Read, Devotional, Journal, Braindump, Stretch, Exercise, Hydrate, Vision, Mission, Purpose

_____
_____
_____
_____

Create

Deliberate Activity, Plan

_____
_____

Communicate

Share or Exchange Information, Ideas, Interact, Network, Touch Base

_____
_____
_____

Celebrate

_____
_____
_____

Hydrate

"Clarity is YOUR Currency" -Nina Obier

My Daily Clarity- 90 Days to Connect.Create.Communicate.Celebrate

Let it FLOW!

"When you step into your brilliance
you spark others to step out in theirs" -Nina Obier

My Daily Clarity- 90 Days to Connect.Create.Communicate.Celebrate

My Daily Clarity

Date: _____

Connect
- Mind
- Body
- Spirit

Meditate, Pray, Read, Devotional, Journal, Braindump, Stretch, Exercise, Hydrate, Vision, Mission, Purpose

Create
Deliberate Activity, Plan

Communicate
Share or Exchange Information, Ideas, Interact, Network, Touch Base

Celebrate

Hydrate

"Clarity is YOUR Currency" -Nina Obier

My Daily Clarity- 90 Days to Connect.Create.Communicate.Celebrate

Let it FLOW!

_____
_____
_____
_____
_____
_____
_____
_____
_____
_____
_____
_____
_____
_____
_____
_____
_____
_____
_____
_____
_____
_____
_____
_____

"When you step into your brilliance
you spark others to step out in theirs" -Nina Obier

My Daily Clarity- 90 Days to Connect.Create.Communicate.Celebrate

My Daily Clarity

Date: _____

Connect — Mind, Body, Spirit

Meditate, Pray, Read, Devotional, Journal, Braindump, Stretch, Exercise, Hydrate, Vision, Mission, Purpose

_____

_____

_____

Create

Deliberate Activity, Plan

_____

_____

_____

Communicate

Share or Exchange Information, Ideas, Interact, Network, Touch Base

_____

_____

_____

Celebrate

_____

_____

_____

Hydrate

"Clarity is YOUR Currency" -Nina Obier

My Daily Clarity- 90 Days to Connect.Create.Communicate.Celebrate

Let it FLOW!

"When you step into your brilliance
you spark others to step out in theirs" -Nina Obier

My Daily Clarity- 90 Days to Connect.Create.Communicate.Celebrate

My Daily Clarity

Date: _____

Connect — Mind, Body, Spirit

Meditate, Pray, Read, Devotional, Journal, Braindump, Stretch, Exercise, Hydrate, Vision, Mission, Purpose

Create

Deliberate Activity, Plan

Communicate

Share or Exchange Information, Ideas, Interact, Network, Touch Base

Celebrate

Hydrate

"Clarity is YOUR Currency" -Nina Obier

My Daily Clarity- 90 Days to Connect.Create.Communicate.Celebrate

Let it FLOW!

"When you step into your brilliance
you spark others to step out in theirs" -Nina Obier

My Daily Clarity- 90 Days to Connect.Create.Communicate.Celebrate

My Daily Clarity

Date: _____

Connect
- Mind
- Body
- Spirit

Meditate, Pray, Read, Devotional, Journal, Braindump, Stretch, Exercise, Hydrate, Vision, Mission, Purpose

Create
Deliberate Activity, Plan

Communicate
Share or Exchange Information, Ideas, Interact, Network, Touch Base

Celebrate

Hydrate

"Clarity is YOUR Currency" -Nina Obier

My Daily Clarity- 90 Days to Connect.Create.Communicate.Celebrate

Let it FLOW!

"When you step into your brilliance
you spark others to step out in theirs" -Nina Obier

My Daily Clarity- 90 Days to Connect.Create.Communicate.Celebrate

My Daily Clarity

Date: _____

Connect
- Mind
- Body
- Spirit

Meditate, Pray, Read, Devotional, Journal, Braindump, Stretch, Exercise, Hydrate, Vision, Mission, Purpose

Create

Deliberate Activity, Plan

Communicate

Share or Exchange Information, Ideas, Interact, Network, Touch Base

Celebrate

Hydrate

"Clarity is YOUR Currency" -Nina Obier

My Daily Clarity- 90 Days to Connect.Create.Communicate.Celebrate

Let it FLOW!

Feeling Foggy? Book a Rapid Results Session

"When you step into your brilliance
you spark others to step out in theirs" -Nina Obier

My Daily Clarity- 90 Days to Connect.Create.Communicate.Celebrate

My Daily Clarity

Date: _____

Connect
- Mind
- Body
- Spirit

Meditate, Pray, Read, Devotional, Journal, Braindump, Stretch, Exercise, Hydrate, Vision, Mission, Purpose

Create
Deliberate Activity, Plan

Communicate
Share or Exchange Information, Ideas, Interact, Network, Touch Base

Celebrate

Hydrate

"Clarity is YOUR Currency" -Nina Obier

My Daily Clarity- 90 Days to Connect.Create.Communicate.Celebrate

It's ALL Good!

I give myself a pat on the back for:

___

I'm feeling so cheerful and blessed:

___

I say YES to:

___

Thank you for the clarity on:

___

"When you change the way you look at things, the things you look at change." -Wayne Dyer

My Daily Clarity- 90 Days to Connect.Create.Communicate.Celebrate

Doodle Page- Color, Mind Map, Imagine, Write Your Favorite Quote/Book/Song/Recipe

Let it FLOW!

"When you step into your brilliance you spark others to step out in theirs" -Nina Obier

My Daily Clarity- 90 Days to Connect.Create.Communicate.Celebrate

My Daily Clarity

Date: _____

Connect
- Mind
- Body
- Spirit

Meditate, Pray, Read, Devotional, Journal, Braindump, Stretch, Exercise, Hydrate, Vision, Mission, Purpose

Create
Deliberate Activity, Plan

Communicate
Share or Exchange Information, Ideas, Interact, Network, Touch Base

Celebrate

Hydrate

"Clarity is YOUR Currency" -Nina Obier

My Daily Clarity- 90 Days to Connect.Create.Communicate.Celebrate

Let it FLOW!

"When you step into your brilliance
you spark others to step out in theirs" -Nina Obier

My Daily Clarity- 90 Days to Connect.Create.Communicate.Celebrate

My Daily Clarity

Date: _____

Connect
- Mind
- Body
- Spirit

Meditate, Pray, Read, Devotional, Journal, Braindump, Stretch, Exercise, Hydrate, Vision, Mission, Purpose

Create

Deliberate Activity, Plan

Communicate

Share or Exchange Information, Ideas, Interact, Network, Touch Base

Celebrate

Hydrate

"Clarity is YOUR Currency" -Nina Obier

My Daily Clarity- 90 Days to Connect.Create.Communicate.Celebrate

Let it FLOW!

_____

"When you step into your brilliance
you spark others to step out in theirs" -Nina Obier

My Daily Clarity- 90 Days to Connect.Create.Communicate.Celebrate

My Daily Clarity

Date: _____

Connect — Mind, Body, Spirit

Meditate, Pray, Read, Devotional, Journal, Braindump, Stretch, Exercise, Hydrate, Vision, Mission, Purpose

Create

Deliberate Activity, Plan

Communicate

Share or Exchange Information, Ideas, Interact, Network, Touch Base

Celebrate

Hydrate

"Clarity is YOUR Currency" -Nina Obier

My Daily Clarity- 90 Days to Connect.Create.Communicate.Celebrate

Let it FLOW!

"When you step into your brilliance
you spark others to step out in theirs" -Nina Obier

My Daily Clarity- 90 Days to Connect.Create.Communicate.Celebrate

My Daily Clarity

Date: _____

Connect — Mind, Body, Spirit

Meditate, Pray, Read, Devotional, Journal, Braindump, Stretch, Exercise, Hydrate, Vision, Mission, Purpose

_____

_____

_____

Create

Deliberate Activity, Plan

_____

_____

_____

Communicate

Share or Exchange Information, Ideas, Interact, Network, Touch Base

_____

_____

_____

Celebrate

_____

_____

_____

Hydrate

"Clarity is YOUR Currency" -Nina Obier

My Daily Clarity- 90 Days to Connect.Create.Communicate.Celebrate

Let it FLOW!

"When you step into your brilliance
you spark others to step out in theirs" -Nina Obier

My Daily Clarity- 90 Days to Connect.Create.Communicate.Celebrate

My Daily Clarity

Date: _____

Connect — Mind, Body, Spirit

Meditate, Pray, Read, Devotional, Journal, Braindump, Stretch, Exercise, Hydrate, Vision, Mission, Purpose

_____
_____
_____
_____

Create

Deliberate Activity, Plan

_____
_____
_____

Communicate

Share or Exchange Information, Ideas, Interact, Network, Touch Base

_____
_____
_____

Celebrate

_____
_____
_____

Hydrate

"Clarity is YOUR Currency" -Nina Obier

My Daily Clarity- 90 Days to Connect.Create.Communicate.Celebrate

Let it FLOW!

"When you step into your brilliance
you spark others to step out in theirs" -Nina Obier

My Daily Clarity- 90 Days to Connect.Create.Communicate.Celebrate

My Daily Clarity

Date: _____

Connect — Mind, Body, Spirit

Meditate, Pray, Read, Devotional, Journal, Braindump, Stretch, Exercise, Hydrate, Vision, Mission, Purpose

_____
_____
_____

Create

Deliberate Activity, Plan

_____
_____

Communicate

Share or Exchange Information, Ideas, Interact, Network, Touch Base

_____
_____
_____

Celebrate

_____
_____
_____

Hydrate

"Clarity is YOUR Currency" -Nina Obier

My Daily Clarity- 90 Days to Connect.Create.Communicate.Celebrate

Let it FLOW!

Need Clarity? Book a Rapid Results Session

"When you step into your brilliance
you spark others to step out in theirs" -Nina Obier

My Daily Clarity- 90 Days to Connect.Create.Communicate.Celebrate

My Daily Clarity

Date: _____

Connect — Mind, Body, Spirit

Meditate, Pray, Read, Devotional, Journal, Braindump, Stretch, Exercise, Hydrate, Vision, Mission, Purpose

_____
_____
_____

Create

Deliberate Activity, Plan

_____
_____

Communicate

Share or Exchange Information, Ideas, Interact, Network, Touch Base

_____
_____
_____

Celebrate

_____
_____
_____

Hydrate

"Clarity is YOUR Currency" -Nina Obier

My Daily Clarity- 90 Days to Connect.Create.Communicate.Celebrate

It's ALL Good!

I give myself a pat on the back for:
_____
_____
_____
_____
_____

I'm feeling so cheerful and blessed:
_____
_____
_____
_____
_____

I say YES to:
_____
_____
_____
_____
_____

Thank you for the clarity on:
_____
_____
_____
_____
_____

"If we wait until we're ready we'll be waiting for the rest of our lives." -Lemony Snicket

My Daily Clarity- 90 Days to Connect.Create.Communicate.Celebrate

Doodle Page- Color, Mind Map, Imagine, Write Your Favorite Quote/Book/Song/Recipe

My Daily Clarity- 90 Days to Connect.Create.Communicate.Celebrate

Let it FLOW!

_____

"When you step into your brilliance
you spark others to step out in theirs" -Nina Obier

My Daily Clarity- 90 Days to Connect.Create.Communicate.Celebrate

My Daily Clarity

Date: _____

Connect — Mind, Body, Spirit

Meditate, Pray, Read, Devotional, Journal, Braindump, Stretch, Exercise, Hydrate, Vision, Mission, Purpose

Create — Deliberate Activity, Plan

Communicate — Share or Exchange Information, Ideas, Interact, Network, Touch Base

Celebrate

Hydrate

"Clarity is YOUR Currency" -Nina Obier

My Daily Clarity- 90 Days to Connect.Create.Communicate.Celebrate

Let it FLOW!

_____
_____
_____
_____
_____
_____
_____
_____
_____
_____
_____
_____
_____
_____
_____
_____
_____
_____
_____
_____
_____
_____
_____
_____

"When you step into your brilliance
you spark others to step out in theirs" -Nina Obier

My Daily Clarity- 90 Days to Connect.Create.Communicate.Celebrate

My Daily Clarity

Date: _____

Connect — Mind, Body, Spirit

Meditate, Pray, Read, Devotional, Journal, Braindump, Stretch, Exercise, Hydrate, Vision, Mission, Purpose

Create

Deliberate Activity, Plan

Communicate

Share or Exchange Information, Ideas, Interact, Network, Touch Base

Celebrate

Hydrate

"Clarity is YOUR Currency" -Nina Obier

Let it FLOW!

"When you step into your brilliance you spark others to step out in theirs" -Nina Obier

My Daily Clarity- 90 Days to Connect.Create.Communicate.Celebrate

My Daily Clarity

Date: _____

Connect — Mind, Body, Spirit

Meditate, Pray, Read, Devotional, Journal, Braindump, Stretch, Exercise, Hydrate, Vision, Mission, Purpose

_____
_____
_____

Create

Deliberate Activity, Plan

_____
_____

Communicate

Share or Exchange Information, Ideas, Interact, Network, Touch Base

_____
_____
_____

Celebrate

_____
_____
_____

Hydrate

"Clarity is YOUR Currency" -Nina Obier

My Daily Clarity- 90 Days to Connect.Create.Communicate.Celebrate

Let it FLOW!

"When you step into your brilliance
you spark others to step out in theirs" -Nina Obier

My Daily Clarity- 90 Days to Connect.Create.Communicate.Celebrate

My Daily Clarity

Date: _____

Connect — Mind, Body, Spirit

Meditate, Pray, Read, Devotional, Journal, Braindump, Stretch, Exercise, Hydrate, Vision, Mission, Purpose

_____
_____
_____

Create

Deliberate Activity, Plan

_____
_____
_____

Communicate

Share or Exchange Information, Ideas, Interact, Network, Touch Base

_____
_____
_____

Celebrate

_____
_____
_____

Hydrate

"Clarity is YOUR Currency" -Nina Obier

Let it FLOW!

"When you step into your brilliance
you spark others to step out in theirs" -Nina Obier

My Daily Clarity- 90 Days to Connect.Create.Communicate.Celebrate

My Daily Clarity

Date: _____

Connect — Mind, Body, Spirit

Meditate, Pray, Read, Devotional, Journal, Braindump, Stretch, Exercise, Hydrate, Vision, Mission, Purpose

_____
_____
_____
_____
_____

Create

Deliberate Activity, Plan

_____
_____

Communicate

Share or Exchange Information, Ideas, Interact, Network, Touch Base

_____
_____
_____

Celebrate

_____
_____
_____

Hydrate

"Clarity is YOUR Currency" -Nina Obier

My Daily Clarity- 90 Days to Connect.Create.Communicate.Celebrate

Let it FLOW!

"When you step into your brilliance
you spark others to step out in theirs" -Nina Obier

My Daily Clarity- 90 Days to Connect.Create.Communicate.Celebrate

My Daily Clarity

Date: _____

Connect
- Mind
- Body
- Spirit

Meditate, Pray, Read, Devotional, Journal, Braindump, Stretch, Exercise, Hydrate, Vision, Mission, Purpose

Create

Deliberate Activity, Plan

Communicate

Share or Exchange Information, Ideas, Interact, Network, Touch Base

Celebrate

Hydrate

"Clarity is YOUR Currency" -Nina Obier

My Daily Clarity- 90 Days to Connect.Create.Communicate.Celebrate

Let it FLOW!

Feeling Stuck? Book a Rapid Results Session

"When you step into your brilliance
you spark others to step out in theirs" -Nina Obier

My Daily Clarity- 90 Days to Connect.Create.Communicate.Celebrate

My Daily Clarity

Date: _____

Connect — Mind, Body, Spirit

Meditate, Pray, Read, Devotional, Journal, Braindump, Stretch, Exercise, Hydrate, Vision, Mission, Purpose

Create

Deliberate Activity, Plan

Communicate

Share or Exchange Information, Ideas, Interact, Network, Touch Base

Celebrate

Hydrate

"Clarity is YOUR Currency" -Nina Obier

My Daily Clarity- 90 Days to Connect.Create.Communicate.Celebrate

It's ALL Good!

I give myself a pat on the back for:
_____
_____
_____
_____
_____

I'm feeling so cheerful and blessed:
_____
_____
_____
_____
_____

I say YES to:
_____
_____
_____
_____
_____

Thank you for the clarity on:
_____
_____
_____
_____

"Don't go through life, grow through life."
-Eric Butterworth

My Daily Clarity- 90 Days to Connect.Create.Communicate.Celebrate

Doodle Page- Color, Mind Map, Imagine, Write Your Favorite Quote/Book/Song/Recipe

My Daily Clarity- 90 Days to Connect.Create.Communicate.Celebrate

Let it FLOW!

"When you step into your brilliance
you spark others to step out in theirs" -Nina Obier

My Daily Clarity- 90 Days to Connect.Create.Communicate.Celebrate

My Daily Clarity

Date: _____

Connect
- Mind
- Body
- Spirit

Meditate, Pray, Read, Devotional, Journal, Braindump, Stretch, Exercise, Hydrate, Vision, Mission, Purpose

_____
_____
_____

Deliberate Activity, Plan

Create

_____
_____

Communicate

Share or Exchange Information, Ideas, Interact, Network, Touch Base

_____
_____
_____

Celebrate

_____
_____
_____

Hydrate

"Clarity is YOUR Currency" -Nina Obier

My Daily Clarity- 90 Days to Connect.Create.Communicate.Celebrate

Let it FLOW!

_____

"When you step into your brilliance
you spark others to step out in theirs" -Nina Obier

My Daily Clarity- 90 Days to Connect.Create.Communicate.Celebrate

My Daily Clarity

Date: _____

Connect
- Mind
- Body
- Spirit

Meditate, Pray, Read, Devotional, Journal, Braindump, Stretch, Exercise, Hydrate, Vision, Mission, Purpose

Create
Deliberate Activity, Plan

Communicate
Share or Exchange Information, Ideas, Interact, Network, Touch Base

Celebrate

Hydrate

"Clarity is YOUR Currency" -Nina Obier

My Daily Clarity- 90 Days to Connect.Create.Communicate.Celebrate

Let it FLOW!

"When you step into your brilliance
you spark others to step out in theirs" -Nina Obier

My Daily Clarity- 90 Days to Connect.Create.Communicate.Celebrate

My Daily Clarity

Date: _____

Connect — Mind, Body, Spirit

Meditate, Pray, Read, Devotional, Journal, Braindump, Stretch, Exercise, Hydrate, Vision, Mission, Purpose

_____
_____
_____

Create

Deliberate Activity, Plan

_____
_____
_____

Communicate

Share or Exchange Information, Ideas, Interact, Network, Touch Base

_____
_____

Celebrate

_____
_____
_____

Hydrate

"Clarity is YOUR Currency" -Nina Obier

Let it FLOW!

"When you step into your brilliance
you spark others to step out in theirs" -Nina Obier

My Daily Clarity- 90 Days to Connect.Create.Communicate.Celebrate

My Daily Clarity

Date: _____

Connect — Mind, Body, Spirit

Meditate, Pray, Read, Devotional, Journal, Braindump, Stretch, Exercise, Hydrate, Vision, Mission, Purpose

Create

Deliberate Activity, Plan

Communicate

Share or Exchange Information, Ideas, Interact, Network, Touch Base

Celebrate

Hydrate

"Clarity is YOUR Currency" -Nina Obier

My Daily Clarity- 90 Days to Connect.Create.Communicate.Celebrate

Let it FLOW!

"When you step into your brilliance
you spark others to step out in theirs" -Nina Obier

My Daily Clarity- 90 Days to Connect.Create.Communicate.Celebrate

My Daily Clarity

Date: _____

Connect — Mind, Body, Spirit

Meditate, Pray, Read, Devotional, Journal, Braindump, Stretch, Exercise, Hydrate, Vision, Mission, Purpose

Create

Deliberate Activity, Plan

Communicate

Share or Exchange Information, Ideas, Interact, Network, Touch Base

Celebrate

Hydrate

"Clarity is YOUR Currency" -Nina Obier

My Daily Clarity- 90 Days to Connect.Create.Communicate.Celebrate

Let it FLOW!

_____

"When you step into your brilliance
you spark others to step out in theirs" -Nina Obier

My Daily Clarity- 90 Days to Connect.Create.Communicate.Celebrate

My Daily Clarity

Date: _____

Connect
- Mind
- Body
- Spirit

Meditate, Pray, Read, Devotional, Journal, Braindump, Stretch, Exercise, Hydrate, Vision, Mission, Purpose

_____

_____

_____

Create

Deliberate Activity, Plan

_____

_____

Communicate

Share or Exchange Information, Ideas, Interact, Network, Touch Base

_____

_____

_____

Celebrate

_____

_____

_____

Hydrate

"Clarity is YOUR Currency" -Nina Obier

My Daily Clarity- 90 Days to Connect.Create.Communicate.Celebrate

Let it FLOW!

Ready For More? Book Rapid Results Session

"When you step into your brilliance
you spark others to step out in theirs" -Nina Obier

My Daily Clarity- 90 Days to Connect.Create.Communicate.Celebrate

My Daily Clarity

Date: _____

Connect — Mind, Body, Spirit

Meditate, Pray, Read, Devotional, Journal, Braindump, Stretch, Exercise, Hydrate, Vision, Mission, Purpose

Create

Deliberate Activity, Plan

Communicate

Share or Exchange Information, Ideas, Interact, Network, Touch Base

Celebrate

Hydrate

"Clarity is YOUR Currency" -Nina Obier

My Daily Clarity- 90 Days to Connect.Create.Communicate.Celebrate

It's ALL Good!

I give myself a pat on the back for:
_____
_____
_____
_____
_____

I'm feeling so cheerful and blessed:
_____
_____
_____
_____
_____

I say YES to:
_____
_____
_____
_____
_____

Thank you for the clarity on:
_____
_____
_____
_____

"The more you praise and celebrate your life, the more there is in life to celebrate." -Oprah Winfrey

My Daily Clarity- 90 Days to Connect.Create.Communicate.Celebrate

Doodle Page- Color, Mind Map, Imagine, Write Your Favorite Quote/Book/Song/Recipe

My Daily Clarity- 90 Days to Connect.Create.Communicate.Celebrate

Let it FLOW!

"When you step into your brilliance
you spark others to step out in theirs" -Nina Obier

My Daily Clarity- 90 Days to Connect.Create.Communicate.Celebrate

My Daily Clarity

Date: _____

Connect — Mind, Body, Spirit

Meditate, Pray, Read, Devotional, Journal, Braindump, Stretch, Exercise, Hydrate, Vision, Mission, Purpose

Deliberate Activity, Plan

Create

Communicate

Share or Exchange Information, Ideas, Interact, Network, Touch Base

Celebrate

Hydrate

"Clarity is YOUR Currency" -Nina Obier

My Daily Clarity- 90 Days to Connect.Create.Communicate.Celebrate

Let it FLOW!

"When you step into your brilliance
you spark others to step out in theirs" -Nina Obier

My Daily Clarity- 90 Days to Connect.Create.Communicate.Celebrate

My Daily Clarity

Date: _____

Connect — Mind, Body, Spirit

Meditate, Pray, Read, Devotional, Journal, Braindump, Stretch, Exercise, Hydrate, Vision, Mission, Purpose

Create

Deliberate Activity, Plan

Communicate

Share or Exchange Information, Ideas, Interact, Network, Touch Base

Celebrate

Hydrate

"Clarity is YOUR Currency" -Nina Obier

My Daily Clarity- 90 Days to Connect.Create.Communicate.Celebrate

Let it FLOW!

"When you step into your brilliance
you spark others to step out in theirs" -Nina Obier

My Daily Clarity- 90 Days to Connect.Create.Communicate.Celebrate

My Daily Clarity

Date: _____

Connect — Mind, Body, Spirit

Meditate, Pray, Read, Devotional, Journal, Braindump, Stretch, Exercise, Hydrate, Vision, Mission, Purpose

Create — Deliberate Activity, Plan

Communicate — Share or Exchange Information, Ideas, Interact, Network, Touch Base

Celebrate

Hydrate

"Clarity is YOUR Currency" -Nina Obier

My Daily Clarity- 90 Days to Connect.Create.Communicate.Celebrate

Let it FLOW!

"When you step into your brilliance
you spark others to step out in theirs" -Nina Obier

My Daily Clarity- 90 Days to Connect.Create.Communicate.Celebrate

My Daily Clarity

Date: _____

Connect — Mind, Body, Spirit

Meditate, Pray, Read, Devotional, Journal, Braindump, Stretch, Exercise, Hydrate, Vision, Mission, Purpose

_____
_____
_____

Create

Deliberate Activity, Plan

_____
_____
_____

Communicate

Share or Exchange Information, Ideas, Interact, Network, Touch Base

_____
_____
_____

Celebrate

_____
_____
_____

Hydrate

"Clarity is YOUR Currency" -Nina Obier

My Daily Clarity- 90 Days to Connect.Create.Communicate.Celebrate

Let it FLOW!

_____

"When you step into your brilliance
you spark others to step out in theirs" -Nina Obier

My Daily Clarity- 90 Days to Connect.Create.Communicate.Celebrate

My Daily Clarity

Date: _____

Connect — Mind, Body, Spirit

Meditate, Pray, Read, Devotional, Journal, Braindump, Stretch, Exercise, Hydrate, Vision, Mission, Purpose

Create

Deliberate Activity, Plan

Communicate

Share or Exchange Information, Ideas, Interact, Network, Touch Base

Celebrate

Hydrate

"Clarity is YOUR Currency" -Nina Obier

My Daily Clarity- 90 Days to Connect.Create.Communicate.Celebrate

Let it FLOW!

"When you step into your brilliance
you spark others to step out in theirs" -Nina Obier

My Daily Clarity - 90 Days to Connect.Create.Communicate.Celebrate

My Daily Clarity

Date: _____

Connect — Mind, Body, Spirit

Meditate, Pray, Read, Devotional, Journal, Braindump, Stretch, Exercise, Hydrate, Vision, Mission, Purpose

_____

_____

_____

Create

Deliberate Activity, Plan

_____

_____

Communicate

Share or Exchange Information, Ideas, Interact, Network, Touch Base

_____

_____

_____

Celebrate

_____

_____

_____

Hydrate

"Clarity is YOUR Currency" -Nina Obier

My Daily Clarity- 90 Days to Connect.Create.Communicate.Celebrate

Let it FLOW!

Celebrate! Book a Rapid Results Session

"When you step into your brilliance you spark others to step out in theirs" -Nina Obier

My Daily Clarity- 90 Days to Connect.Create.Communicate.Celebrate

My Daily Clarity

Date: _____

Connect
- Mind
- Body
- Spirit

Meditate, Pray, Read, Devotional, Journal, Braindump, Stretch, Exercise, Hydrate, Vision, Mission, Purpose

_____
_____
_____

Create

Deliberate Activity, Plan

_____
_____

Communicate

Share or Exchange Information, Ideas, Interact, Network, Touch Base

_____
_____
_____

Celebrate

_____
_____
_____

Hydrate

"Clarity is YOUR Currency" -Nina Obier

My Daily Clarity- 90 Days to Connect.Create.Communicate.Celebrate

It's ALL Good!

I give myself a pat on the back for:

_____
_____
_____
_____
_____

I'm feeling so cheerful and blessed:

_____
_____
_____
_____
_____

I say YES to:

_____
_____
_____
_____
_____

Thank you for the clarity on:

_____
_____
_____
_____

"Being your true self begins when your inner attitude matches your outward actions."
-Nina Obier

My Daily Clarity- 90 Days to Connect.Create.Communicate.Celebrate

Doodle Page- Color, Mind Map, Imagine, Write Your Favorite Quote/Book/Song/Recipe

My Daily Clarity- 90 Days to Connect.Create.Communicate.Celebrate

www.ninaobier.com

My Daily Clarity- 90 Days to Connect.Create.Communicate.Celebrate

"Your life does not get better by chance, it gets better by change" -Unknown

(turn the page and REFLECT)

My Daily Clarity- 90 Days to Connect.Create.Communicate.Celebrate

YES, Let's Do a Braindump, Get it ALL out of Your Head
Date:_____(how do you feel, what's going right, what's different since you started this journey)

_____
_____
_____
_____
_____
_____
_____
_____
_____
_____
_____
_____
_____
_____
_____
_____
_____
_____
_____
_____
_____
_____
_____
_____
_____
_____
_____
_____

My Daily Clarity- 90 Days to Connect.Create.Communicate.Celebrate

(Keep Going) Date:_____

My Daily Clarity- 90 Days to Connect.Create.Communicate.Celebrate

www.ninaobier.com

My Daily Clarity - 90 Days to Connect.Create.Communicate.Celebrate

YOU DID IT!- It's time to reflect. Who are you BEING? What are you DOING? What do you HAVE? What's NEXT?

BEING
___

DOING
___

HAVE
___

What's NEXT?
___

"Who you become is infinitely more important than what you do, or what you have."
-Matthew Kelly

My Daily Clarity- 90 Days to Connect.Create.Communicate.Celebrate

www.ninaobier.com

My Daily Clarity- 90 Days to Connect.Create.Communicate.Celebrate

ABOUT THE AUTHOR

Nina Obier is an Exceptional Listener, Author, Freedom Facilitator and Training & Development Specialist in Human Connection. Her personal mission is to be a lively, loving, leader who is leaving a legacy focused on faith, family, fun and freedom. Best known for her positive energy, great listening skills, and her ability to simplify things for others, her passion for serving others shines through when she's training, as does her desire for her clients to have fun.

Throughout her life, Nina has always been a leader. Whether at her corporate hotel job at Hyatt Hotels International, her training position at the Federal Reserve, within her Direct Selling business for 15 years, or with the Softball Booster Club, she consistently created an environment of success. The challenges that leadership presented further developed Nina's strengths in relationship building, professionalism, organization, and communication. It's these life lessons that Nina uses to inspire her audiences to help them grow. Nina focuses on developing the leader within ourselves, through training on vision, attitude, and communication.

Along with her degree in hospitality management, Nina's specific speaker qualifications include over 20 years of training and development experience in Leadership, Time Management, Customer Service, and Communication. She is a certified speaker, trainer and coach with the John Maxwell Team. Nina has served as Master of Ceremony for two Regional Direct Sellers conventions with 900 attendees, breakout Speaker at National Direct Sellers conference with 4000 attendees, and appeared in Empowering Women Magazine.

Nina is the founder of Success in Leadership and has 20 years experience as a Freedom Facilitator. She is the published author of Listen.Learn.Love.Lead - 40 Simple Messages for an #inspiredlife. The title represents more than just a book she wrote. Instead, it is a mantra she promotes.

Made in the USA
Columbia, SC
10 November 2018